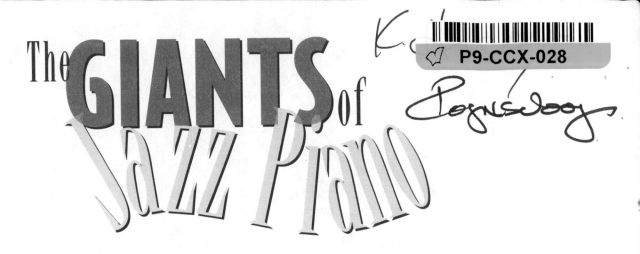

The GIANTS of Jazz Piano

Project Manager: Tony Esposito
Cover Design: Odalis Soto

© 1996 WARNER BROS. PUBLICATIONS
All Rights Reserved

From the M-G-M Musical Production "HOLLYWOOD HOTEL"

Blue Moon

Lyric by
LORENZ HART

Music by
RICHARD RODGERS
Piano Solo Arr. by
ART TATUM

Blue Moon - 2 - 1

Bluette

By
DAVE BRUBECK

1st Improvisation

Bluette - 5 - 2

6

2rd Improvisation

3rd Improvisation

4th Improvisation

Birmingham Breakdown

By
DUKE ELLINGTON

Birmingham Breakdown - 3 - 1

Blue Rondo A La Turk

By DAVE BRUBECK

Blue Rondo A La Turk - 10 - 1

Blue Rondo A La Turk - 10 - 2

14

16

18

Blue Rondo A La Turk - 10 - 7

Blue Rondo A La Turk - 10 - 8

Blue Rondo A La Turk - 10 - 10

Coquette

Words by
GUS KAHN

Music by
CARMEN LOMBARDO and JOHN GREEN

Coquette - 2 - 1

Coquette - 2 - 2

The Duke

By
DAVE BRUBECK

With a relaxed beat

The Duke - 3 - 1

CODA

From "THE AMERICANIZATION OF EMILY"

Emily

Words by
JOHNNY MERCER

JOHNNY MANDEL

Moderately

Emily - 9 - 1

Emily - 9 - 2

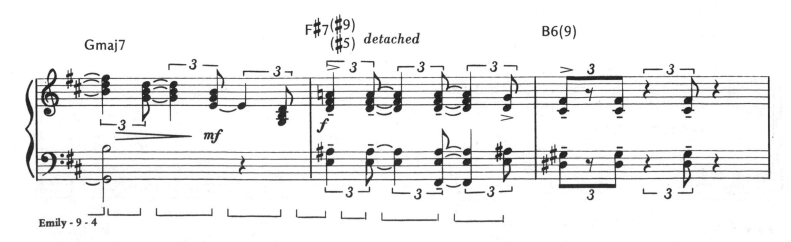

Emily - 9 - 5

a touch of pedal - - - - - - - - - -

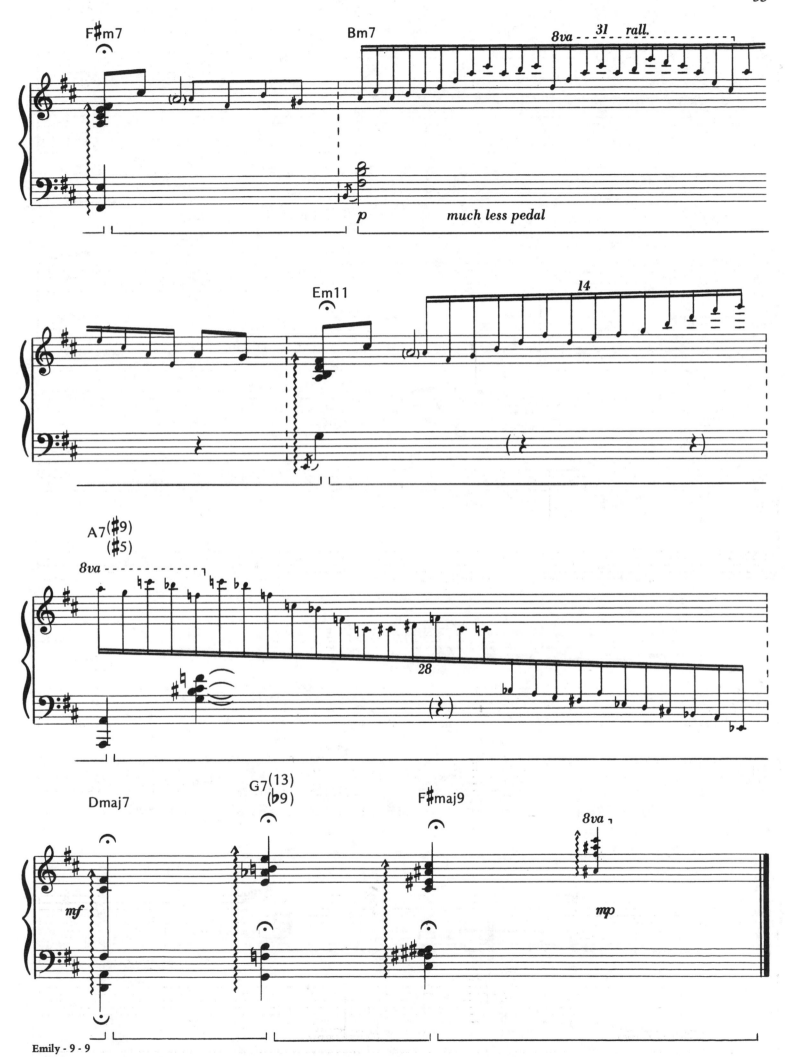

Echoes Of Harlem

By
DUKE ELLINGTON

Echoes of Harlem - 2 - 1

For All We Know

Words by
SAM M. LEWIS

Music by
J. FRED COOTS

For All We Know - 6 - 4

I'll Never Be The Same

Piano Solo Arr. by
ART TATUM

By GUS KAHN,
MATT MALNECK and
FRANK SIGNORELLI

Moderato

I'll Never Be the Same - 2 - 1

I'm In The Mood For Love

Piano Solo Arr. by
Arranged by ART TATUM

Words and Music by
JIMMY McHUGH and
DOROTHY FIELDS

I'm in the Mood Solo Love - 2 - 1

I'm in the Mood for Love - 2 - 2

Ja-Da

Words and Music by
BOB CARLETON
Piano Solo Arr. by
ART TATUM

Ja-Da - 2 - 1

Get Happy

Words and Music by
HAROLD ARLEN and TED KOEHLER

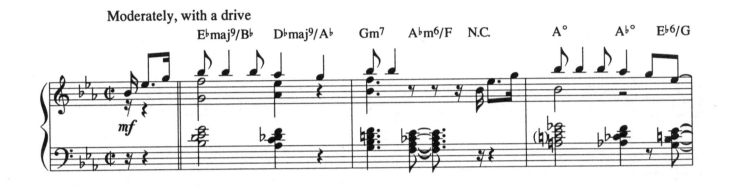

Get Happy - 3 - 1

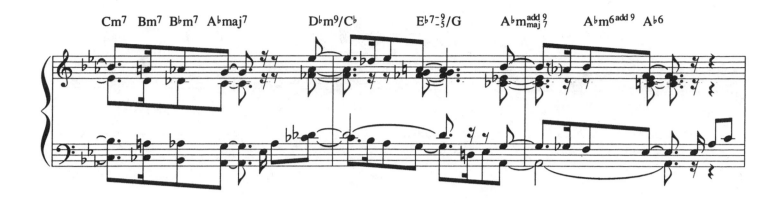

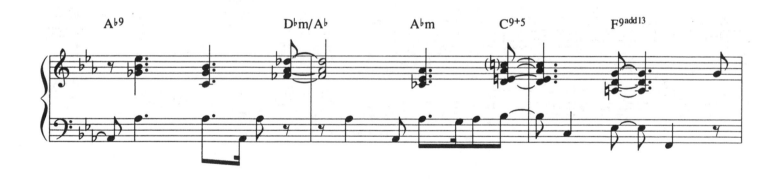

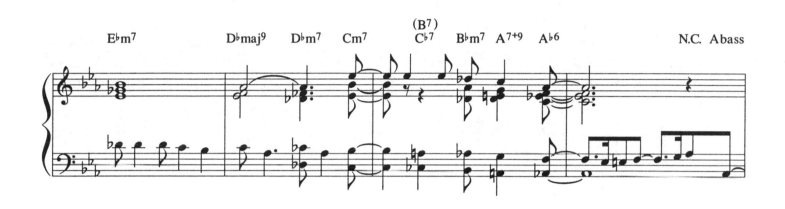

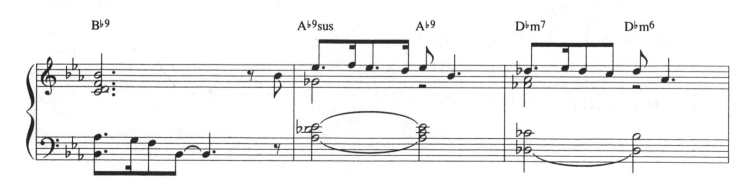

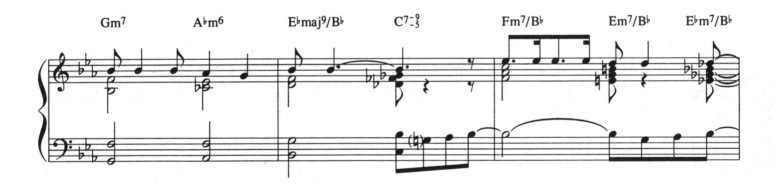

Fast Life

By
DAVE BRUBECK

Fast Life - 7 - 1

Fast Life - 7 - 5

From the 20th Century-Fox Motion Picture "LAURA"

Laura

Lyric by
JOHNNY MERCER

Music by
DAVID RAKSIN

Laura - 6 - 1

*Jazz waltz feeling

Laura - 6 - 2

Laura - 6 - 3

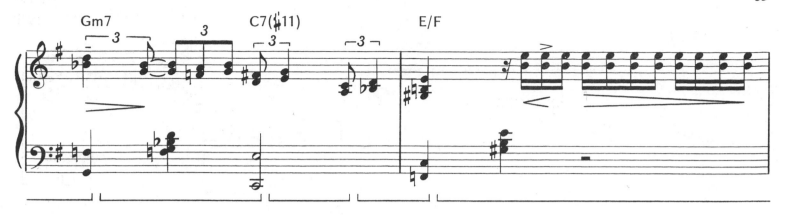

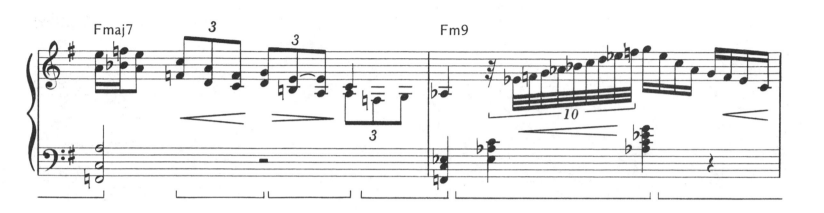

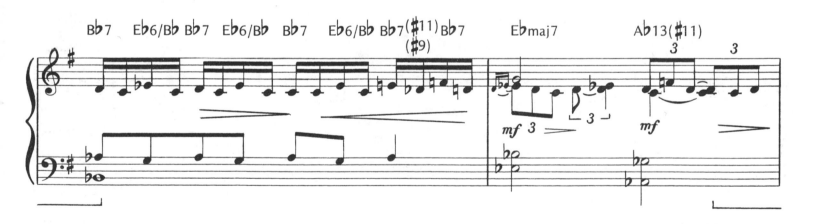

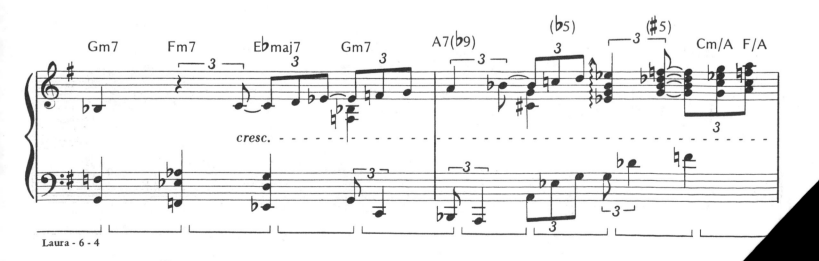

Laura - 6 - 4

Fascinating Rhythm

Music and Lyrics by
GEORGE GERSHWIN and IRA GERSHWIN

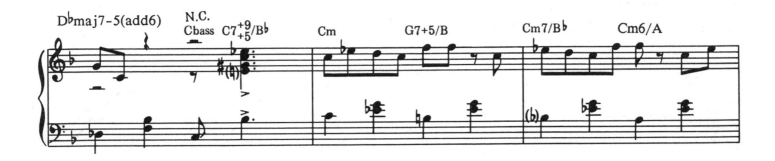

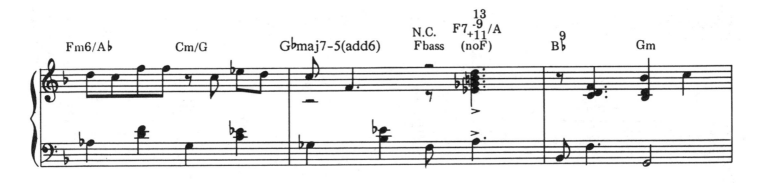

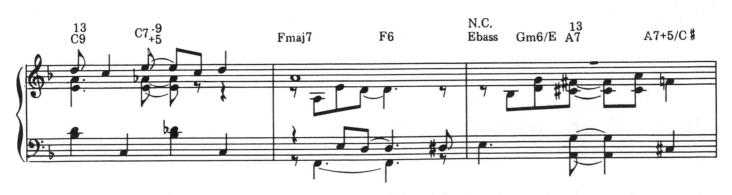

Fascinating Rhythm - 3 - 1

If You Could See Me Now

Lyric by
CARL SIGMAN

Music by
TAD DAMERON

If You Could See Me Now - 5 - 1

Lullaby In Rhythm

Piano Solo Arr. by
ART TATUM

By BENNY GOODMAN,
EDGAR SAMPSON,
CLARENCE PROFIT and
WALTER HIRSCH

Lullaby in Rhythm - 2 - 1

The Jeep Is Jumpin'

By DUKE ELLINGTON
and JOHNNY HODGES

The Jeep Is Jumpin' - 3 - 1

The Jeep Is Jumpin' - 3 - 3

A Last Request

By
DAVID BENOIT

A Last Request - 5 - 1

Liza
(All the Clouds'll Roll Away)

Words by
IRA GERSHWIN and GUS KAHN

Music by
GEORGE GERSHWIN

Easy tempo. with a beat

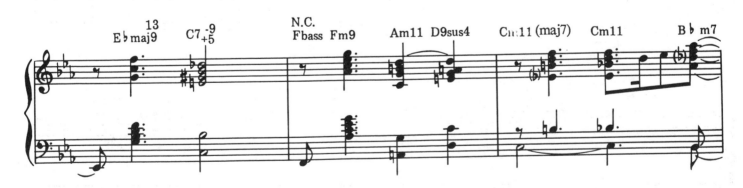

Liza - 3 - 1

Liza - 3 - 2

Lullaby Of Birdland

Words by
GEORGE DAVID WEISS

Music by
GEORGE SHEARING

Lullaby of Birdland - 3 - 1

88

Lullaby of Birdland - 3 - 3

M.W.A.
(Musicians with Attitude)

By DAVID BENOIT,
NATHAN EAST and
MARCEL EAST

M.W.A. (Musicians with Attitude) - 7 - 1

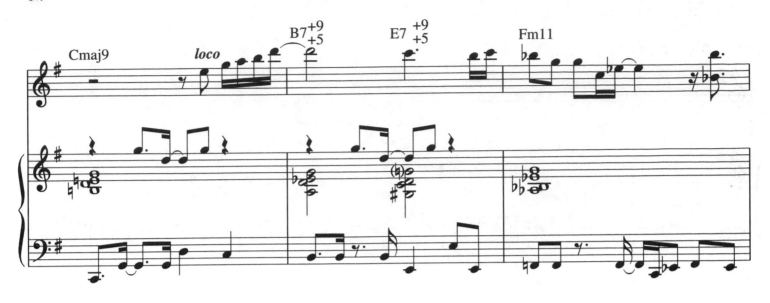

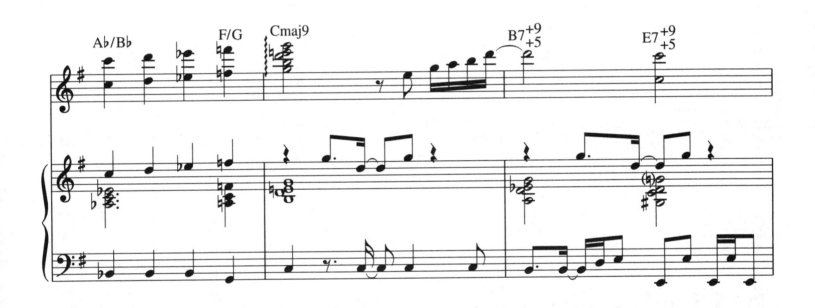

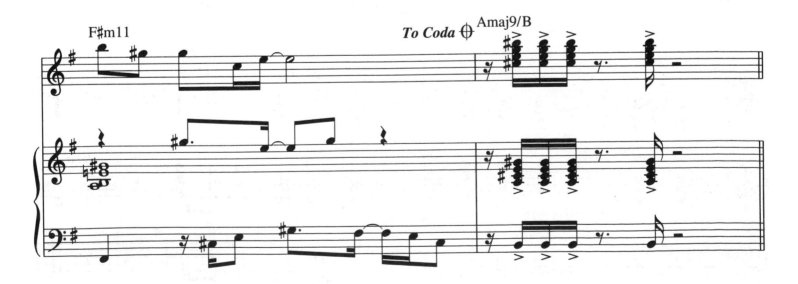

From the M-G-M Motion Picture "GREEN DOLPHIN STREET"

On Green Dolphin Street

Lyrics by
NED WASHINGTON

Music by
BRONISLAU KAPER

On Green Dolphin Street - 3 - 1

On Green Dolphin Street - 3 - 2

On Green Dolphin Street - 3 - 3

From the Motion Picture "THE WIZARD OF OZ"

Over The Rainbow

Lyric by
E. Y. HARBURG

Music by
HAROLD ARLEN

Over The Rainbow - 2 - 1

Rockin' In Rhythm

By DUKE ELLINGTON,
IRVING MILLS and
HARRY CARNEY

Rockin' in Rhythm - 4 - 1

Rockin' in Rhythm - 4 - 4

6-String Poet

By
DAVID BENOIT

The Shadow Of Your Smile

(Love Theme from ''The Sandpiper'')

Lyric by
PAUL FRANCIS WEBSTER

Music by
JOHNNY MANDEL

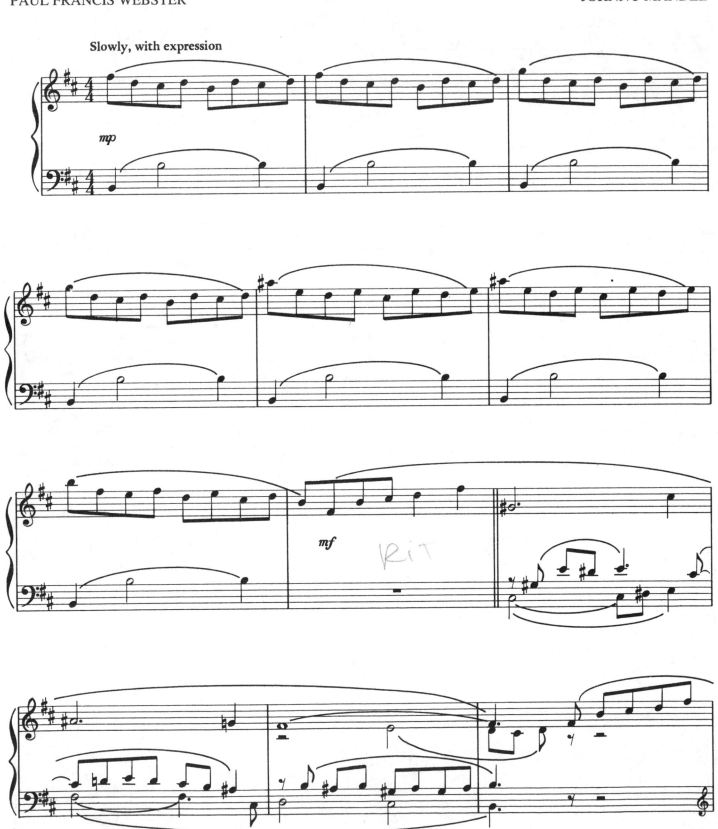

The Shadow Of Your Smile - 3 - 1

The Shadow Of Your Smile - 3 - 2

Skylark

Words by
JOHNNY MERCER

Music by
HOAGY CARMICHAEL

Skylark - 3 - 1

112

Skylark - 3 - 2

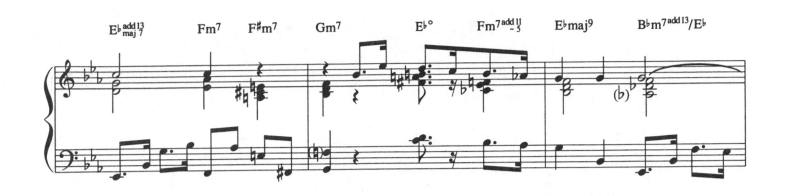

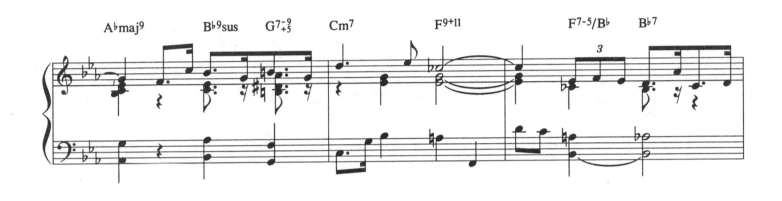

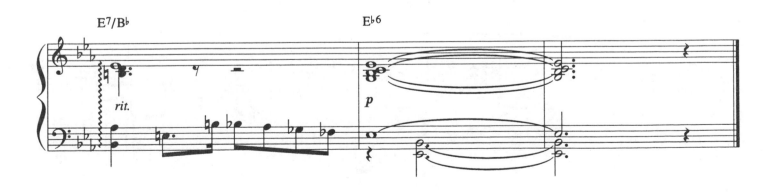

Featured in Dwight Deere Wiman's Musical Comedy "I MARRIED AN ANGEL"

Spring Is Here

Words by
LORENZ HART

Music by
RICHARD RODGERS

Spring Is Here - 2 - 1

Stompin' At The Savoy

Lyric by
ANDY RAZAF
Piano Solo Arr. by
ART TATUM

Music by
BENNY GOODMAN, CHICK WEBB and
EDGAR SAMPSON

Stompin' at the Savoy - 2 - 1

The Summer Knows
(Theme from ''Summer of '42'')

Words by
MARILYN and ALAN BERGMAN

Music by
MICHEL LEGRAND

Straight 8th's ♩ = ca. 63

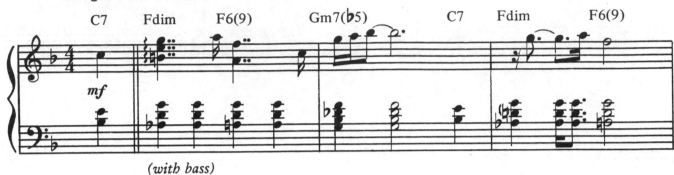

(with bass)

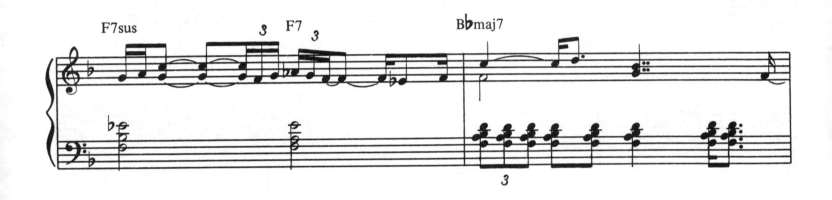

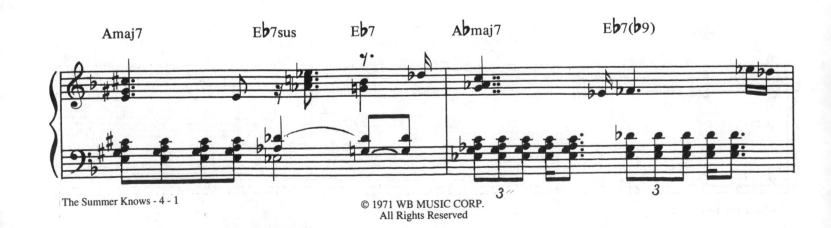

The Summer Knows - 4 - 1

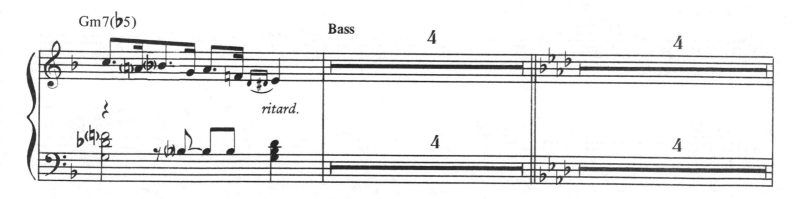

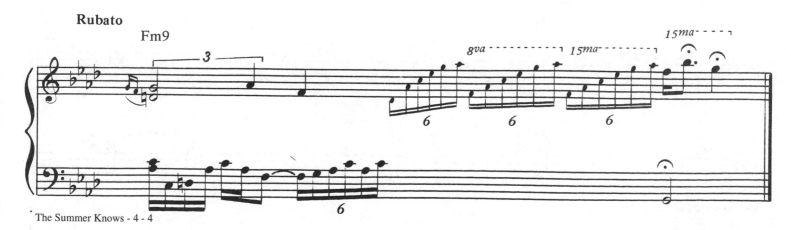

Take Five

By
PAUL DESMOND

Moderately fast ♩=176

Take Five - 4 - 1

Take Five - 4 - 2

Take Five - 4 - 3

Take Five - 4 - 4

Take 6

By
DAVID BENOIT

Take 6 - 2 - 1

What Is This Thing Called Love?

Words and Music by
COLE PORTER

Up tempo (bebop)

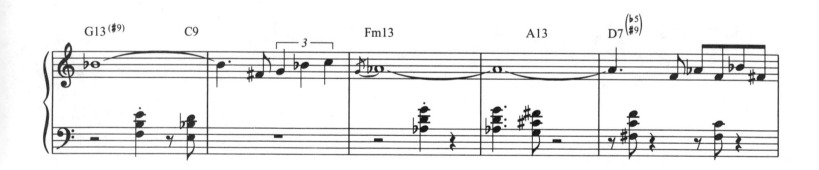

What Is This Thing Called Love – 12 – 1

What Is This Thing Called Love – 12 – 2

Piano Solo

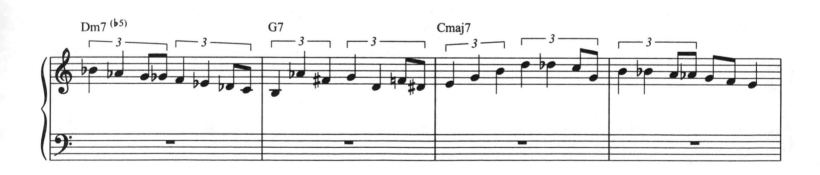

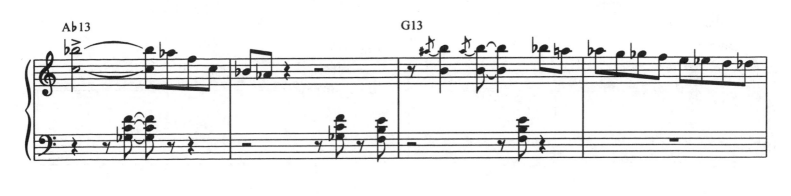

What Is This Thing Called Love – 12 – 4

What Is This Thing Called Love – 12 – 5

What Is This Thing Called Love – 12 – 6

134

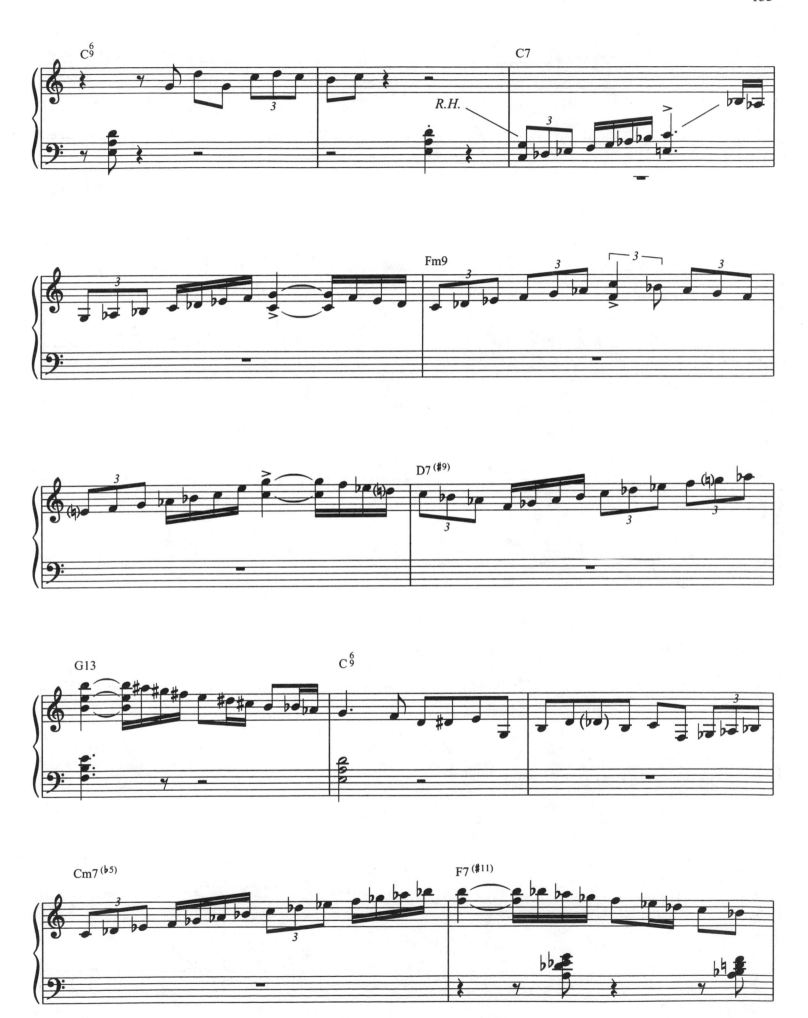

What Is This Thing Called Love – 12 – 10

138

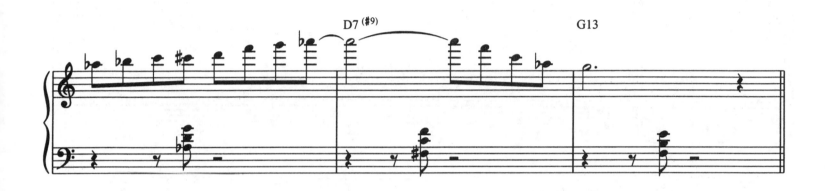

What Is This Thing Called Love – 12 – 12

Sombody Loves Me

Words by
B.G. DeSYLVA and BALLARD MACDONALD

Music by
GEORGE GERSHWIN

Somebody Loves Me - 3 - 1

Summer Song

Lyrics by
IOLA & DAVE BRUBECK

Music by
DAVE BRUBECK

Summer Song - 7 - 1

*Pedal each chord at the instant of its release.

A Time For Love

Words by
PAUL FRANCIS WEBSTER

Music by
JOHNNY MANDEL

A Time for Love - 11 - 8